Manual Random Hill

Patrick Williams

NINE MILE BOOKS

Publisher: Nine Mile Art Corp.
Editors: Bob Herz, Stephen Kuusisto, Andrea Scarpino
Art Editor Emeritus: Whitney Daniels
Cover Art: Mark Mulroney
Photo credit: Dan Perez De La Garza

Nine Mile Books is an imprint of Nine Mile Art Corp.

The publishers gratefully acknowledge support of the New York State Council on the Arts with the support of Governor Andrew M. Cuomo and the New York State Legislature. We also acknowledge support of the County of Onondaga and CNY Arts through the Tier Three Project Support Grant Program. We have also received significant support from the Central New York Community Foundation. This publication would not have been possible without the generous support of these groups. We are very grateful to them all.

ISBN: 978-1-7377880-0-3

Acknowledgements

I would like to acknowledge with gratitude the editors of the following journals, in which many of these poems first appeared: *3:AM Magazine, A Quiet Courage, Bennington Review, Birds' Thumb, The Birds We Piled Loosely, Burning House Press, The Collapsar, Glitter Mob, Heavy Feather Review, Hot Metal Bridge, Incessant Pipe, The Mackinac, Moonchild, Nine Mile Magazine, Noble / Gas Quarterly, The Occulum, Posit, Prelude, Pretty Owl Poetry, Public Pool, Reality Beach, Right Hand Pointing, Sea Foam Magazine, SOFTBLOW, Vayavya, Vinyl, and Word Riot.*

Contents

I

Cinepak

An empty dossier gets you kitchen sinked.
You absorb loose photons like a new coat
of primer. You eat clean light and could
forever. Like matte boot-black. Like long
days spent brushing red-rot off books. Each
pixel-width disclosure reveals a bit of your
fingerprint. Let's learn, let's lean on glissando,
let's let some same sounds phase. Let's switch
on our remote looks when things get heavy.
All those bee-stung children know it now.
Some are willing to drop refs over yellow-cards.
One shot his younger sister; his firearm read
full toy. There are probably enough hulks in this
already, but really: do you. I know it's tempting
to grouse the interface. I prefer to putty-color it.

Automatic Writing

At our worst press conferences
whatever spotlit official will pause
and step back to let the wind rush
over a bouquet of hot mics and roar
revenge. Offscreen, a thousand
automatic shutter bursts whisper
yes, yes. During marginal moments
in these live feeds, you catch staffers
passing with clipboards, anxiously
orchestrating their uplinks. But we
must conjure the hum of the newsvan
antennae telescoping up and down so
often. That's the text we should read
together. We should study every lull,
subject it to our own psychography.

The Official Jam of the Summer is the Startup Chime in my Hearing Aids

In a worklife soundworld of mostly whispers
or a golden hour ample of data center serenade,
the shape of an old brand's roadsign is far too
faded to claim. I sat in that chamber thinking
I'd been expertly emperor's-new-clothes'd,
or I was auditioning isolated oscillator tracks
from an unreleased 60s Silver Apples joint. I sat
still saying only *yes*, but less often than expected,
to some tape hiss. So, when as a child I was shaken
from deep flow; dismissed from pre-K color time
for comforting myself with a low dronehum
of childgroan, teachers told me I set the others
off their ideas; out in the hall, half-an-hourish.
Believe me, I kept quiet after that. Decades later
someone clued me on how to E.Q. in worlds of tiny
foci, how not to drown a larger one out. Someone
told me it rests in a jar. Listen, remember what
a delicate kind of feeling it is, a sense of fresh distance
if only from within. I didn't; hadn't tried. Now there's a new
chime in to hide the old, to secret-share, a couple
of tubes to hover together, to stem the lemniscate.

Generic

for Lexapro

I lied about having houseplants
in a conversation about having
children. I also lied about birds:
Every loose feather you ever see
comes from a different sick bird.
A bird with a different sickness.
The feather's a symbol for each's
uniqueness. But they mostly fall
from a single bird; wind-washed into
public corners like dander behind doors.
In a brutalist cube of walls and stairs
a man with a fresh black eye asks me
Do you know the name of this street?
I shake my head; I don't. *You better*
learn the name of this street, he
threatens, as he staggers away.
The nearby retromarket in decline
sells cameras, the ones they ceased
producing film for just now. The tram's
right there, so there's foot traffic, but it's
also very cold. The ice cream parlor
closed. Your ransomware reminds me
every idea has a location and address.
It reminds me we are so special
because we each have something
inside that no one else can see,
a many-feathered thing to slowly
destroy that no one else will know is gone.

Manual Random Hill

The sediment of our sweat is profound
privilege, an oblique form of fortune.
We painted our portrait in petroleum
jelly together. Its surface lasted four
hours, but beneath it: more like forever.
Who forced your fall in traffic's path?
A scraped palm will always look filthy.
But ours are never truly filthy, that much
is clear. You & I are merely squatters
on the tiniest parcel of joint & muscle
pain. Let's savor our common affection
for throwback diaeresis in *The New Yorker*.
What else could make a term like *reënlist*
even briefly beautiful to either one of us?
In our yard, each new bite's a symptom,
each squeal's a boosted song hurled up
to our friends who fill the cheapest seats,
gracious as the undersampled fanfare
that blasts each time the lotto box pays out.

Leave Me Your Slide Rule

Static charges are given an effective path
to the ground thanks to the strip of plastic
warming in your loafer. Something to prevent
the snap death of supercomputers who hum
and crunch as we walk among them, you
explained. I knew it then: to live with such
vulnerability demanded systemic finesse
I'd never muster. I mean, imagine catching
hell for all that data's fluky ruin. Your every
working moment militarized, each day built
of spillable secrets future you'd wish he never
had to know. *Think, Smash!* is your thought balloon
in that college-era caricature, pencil behind ear.
You are the *ne plus ultra* of operations research.

Your Kind Attention Please

A children's book should not reveal
our planet to hurtle forever in a corkscrew
motion. Or any objects to move in two
or more directions at once. Just like you
should not tell me the vacation spot
I mention was mostly destroyed by last
month's floods. We already sent the deposit.
The clever food and beverage pairings
are lost on most patrons as they behold
your dinky illusions. Some have even left
their over-cushioned barstools to marvel
at the cardboard box of pale deer bones
carefully placed on the lip of the stage.

Behavior Flows

There was an error in the extended play.
The actors had to change their names.
Called in sick, slept in late, sat on stoops
collecting landing planes. That meteorite
chunk they found? Yeah, I say don't go near it
before it's boxed & bulletproofed. Let's catalog
our sign-offs, let's say them each again.
So often I think they just belong to me.
I just looked at my hands for the first time.
I just told myself *don't think of anything*.
Glory be to the fallout, glory be to the bomb.
Help me find a tufted sofa. Sing me the tune
of kiln-baked wood. Give me an earful
of your star text. I need it for this lawsuit.

That the Lake Would Still Be Frozen
Had Not Occurred to Me

A pool deck mosaic says *hurry up and chill*
somewhere under there. Remember, their father
slept in the truckbed so he wouldn't hallucinate
another jungle war. I had a tent by the toilets,
pitched half on an anthill. It smelled like the spot
where we'd pull honeysuckle from a face-flush bush
ripe with all the alleyway trash. If I had bare feet
I might remember the island, the thick thorns
we crushed just to reach the beach. I might have
seen the sand. The sun is out and the people
are eager, but the lake is dead as a dream.

Tinnitus News

We are too unfixed. Imagine
our psychodynamics without
a real hearer. We had thunder.
Flowwise, we had it down. But
there's a certain clinking noise,
something slowly swirling, like
the woman who bellydances
at everything in town. It's in
the wakes of modern boats,
the jets that dry our hands so
faintly. It's in applause. It's in
the recording of synthetic birds
they blast to scare actual birds
away from where we park our cars.
Someone is calling, but really,
who picks up the phone anymore?

I'm a Sleepwalking Cheetah with a Heart Full of Lip Balm

We were ultra purple and also so for real.
In the binge harvest, we got it straight
from the source. We made things meaningless
so meaning then could come. Watch us whittle
ugly urges. Watch us tabulate the inky costs.
Good Lord, I think you could have waited
at least until we hit that next text stop.
We look up at the new reflective roadsign
typeface: *All the world's a forgotten boy.*
We tune in to the weather band and listen
to a poem of pure joy written by police.

II

New Telegraphy

Forget those stylish communiqués
shilling synthetic facial hair and framed
giclées of suburban drugstore aisles.
If you succeed, you will soon bask in glory.

In this method, what you eventually learn
is that you are the instrument.
Most of the variance is explained
by you. Try wishing that away.

When we share line-of-sight, you'll realize.
I am a famous actor's skeleton.
You know him, he's talking aliens
on video loop at the Duty Free.

I am all the unenclosed space
in Shannon's *Schematic Diagram*
of a General Communication System.
That's figure one in the original text.

In our version, most of the boxes have
been replaced with latex horror masks.
Where once were one-way arrows
now are knotty bootlaces.

In the center, the small nameless box
does not change. It is our index.
It is our compass rose. Remember, it's eight-
to-one bits of English text to entropy.

You will also learn not to mention
something's *validity* since we don't
really use that term, despite what
you have probably read. It's suspect.

I am the instrument. I am suspect.
I am the season's last snowball,
saved in the freezer until it's clear
and far too hard to dream of throwing.

Ill Affordances

Always open files of this type.
If you're lucky, it'll glitch out
six facsimiles, each one addressed
to you. Given time, they'll arrive loose
by post, assuming minimal packet loss.

I will continue to blame my parents
for these frequent namespace errors.
Most families' cupboards are bare.
Mrs. Kim explains how it changed her:
Y'all, she said one night at the Blue & Gold,
*I totally just dropped my phone
in the toilet.* Reply all, in unison, *Again?*

It is a massive inconvenience to allow
engineers to touch what they contrive.
It is also too expensive to hire those
who have driven cars to build them.
Heavy mathematics in the air are
to blame. All our favorite jokes are
based on someone's offensive Wi-Fi ID.

Picture a miniature railroad set. Its toy
machines are churning, little lights blinking,
but all the tiny people are deadly still.
There is no need to assume a new tableau.
You should see the brilliant meanings
today's teens encode in something dull
like this. Bobby's chat status is always *PAINT*.
I made a note to remember that one.

This Reagent Tablet Looks Like a Cert
I Totally Want to Eat It

I know what's in the humid sacks of garbage
behind the florist's shop. At night I walked
quickly and woke the vending machines.
The streets are slick in these memories,

like in films, where crews work to keep them
wet. Obvious things happen to bodies like ours
and unlike ours every day. It's how the West
wasn't won. We've known all this since yesteryear.

For effect, let's cut on form. Let's do
all sixteen dances. Let's unsee the weapon
in the FedEx Logo. Let's ignore the
I'm in my cups in my cups. I'll go first.

Let's watch the ice caps make history, let's
listen to the glaciers calve. Let's inhabit questions
so scary no one with open eyes can ask.
When you look at me I feel like a newborn

mini drone tangled tightly in your sister's hair.
It's a problem that has become all too
common. I hear homemade videos are the best
approach to learning how to free me.

We're in the coat check line at fucking
Irving Plaza again. We climb slowly
the broken stairs. The bus shelters

are thick with layers of missing folks.

In lounge and package, in pattern and act:
just know that when I write *Take care*,
what I mean you to read is *survive*,
Survive survive survive survive survive.

A Magnet Is the Opposite of A Bomb
But What If You Are Both

Per your request I dropped
the window-stunned corpse
of the first oriole we've seen
into the galvanized step-can out front.

We were wrong about the natural
laws; sound and motion are not
the same thing. We pause and see
something entering or leaving

the frame: we can't agree.
We ignore the categories in
anticipation of their collapse.
It's mud or it's mist, a fog

across the surface of the lake.
It's been years since I took photos
of any Ferris wheel I could, from roads
and waterways, an amusement graveyard

near Cheraw; they're all blurred.
Let me read you this list
of megafauna gone extinct.
You will want to live in it

with me. Let's petroglyph,
let's build a new Atlantis now,
before we're ill-suited to smoothness.

Let's really underscore our rural allure.

Consider this my audition
to DJ the subaquatic soundsystem
that revitalized the dying coral reef
if only for an evening.

New Age Downloads

The city stares, the state tunes in.
What's most sharable is born
on chyron crawls or in the initial pause
of an unplanned voicemail. The bent
license plate from a Peugeot Citroën
speeds through early sprawl
bolted to another car.

For many years I didn't want anyone
to know when I slept. If they telephoned
early, I'd act awake. Technically, I was.
But there is shame in doing what bodies
do; a shame in their numbers.

Thanks to the Plastic Age Anniversary,
everyone can control-f their codenames
through any number of relevant leaks.
We hallucinate multiple doppelgängers.
We come alive in pools of cherry-
picked queries, tout de suite.

I grasp a sack of hot fries and watch
a longish Elliot Gould medium shot
on a silent screen at the thruway plaza.
I wait for something to load.

A purported crisis actor arrives in a Cutlass
to paint my portrait out of focus;
I pose in front of a Quartet whiteboard
simply dripping with psychedelic riddles.

Who erased *The Basement Tapes*?
Who'll powerwash the tennis courts?
Who pulled back the blackout drapes?
Who'll re-reinvent motorsports?

North Texas is our secret handshake:
Remember Love Field? I blurt for cred.
Next time, I'm going to collect my personal
effects from the rental car with authority;
I'm told I've got a collector's eye.

I leave footprints in foam and sea oats.
I destroy the oldest dunes. *After seven years,*
I hear a woman whisper *I'm finally sick*
enough to go in front of the board.

So there was a dustup re: corpse paint. Or a
souvenir from Biosphere II. We know what's
saved because it has a name. We don't know
who saved it, because he deleted his account.

We notice a new glow from the neighbors:
a glimpse of their exotic tank.
At midday, they inform for the beat cop
whose mother used to live next door.

Watch me showroom something expensive.
Watch me bankroll a bombastic void. I only ask
that you alert the appropriate authorities
if you're the one whose new tattoo alone
is supposed to remind us all to breathe.

Our Loop

You know how she can
roll with dives so long
as your strongest pitch
pushes any unsavory
metadata into the bokeh?

The real trick is to locate
whole evenings within districts
where even the cleanest
dérailleurs are impermissible.

It's there we dine again, pairwise
in soft pink noise, on the tender
sacrament of our favorite fiction.

Rental Period

Borrow a quarter and press
your face to the steel. Steady
the scope on the ramps and lifts
at thirteen degrees. That's left.

The anxious ticking stands for time,
the silence for *it's up*, for *even
the iris of this soda straw of sense
is too much to take in for long.*

Face the queue of other tourists.
Watch them pull what they can
of moments-older peaks before
each lease on the gaze expires.

Her Pose

Pointing at a single wrinkle
in at least a decade's
bulk of dusty candlemelt.

A hectare of knotted rope
gets the same treatment,
but with flash this time.

Look, she says, *I found*
something little in this.
It's a gift for you.

Soft Construction

Clear your mind of every CEO,
all your loved ones
& zeros. Play the music they play

for you in the waiting room.
The MRI, the CAT scan,
all the things you think

you own. When I did, I woke up
a winner: bedside, the thick book
of codes we used to make

everyone else say hello.
There's link rot in extropia,
there's telltale teenish gloom.

There's more growing
in the gutters than the garden
or the lawn. They call this thing a home.

Make It Out to Cash

Don't seethe
until you are seething.

Per pool a person
& a machine
with the same name

have inherited the earth:
oh how princelings will praise them!

There is never a readout
only a paystub.

There is never an address
only an inkling.

There is never a finger
only a photo array.

The only currency is time.

Let's break the lock
on the ladder that gets you
to the roof of the McDonalds.

Let's sit up
there & seethe.
It's time to seethe now.

Dead Air is an Impossible Crime

Think about the radio. Think about Unalaska.
Think about all the prisoners hearing one-way
messages meant for other prisoners; the reverse
of that song those two mice sang about the sky.

Our oldest sets fed on the luckiest fragments
of an untrustworthy spectrum of static
you couldn't pause a warm dial on for long. Apt to
drift, nudged in each untouchable breeze, jostled off
mark whenever some sleepy relay tech's trip out
for coffee cooled the transmission machinery.

The buttons you recall punching are grubby
teeth in the dash of my father's old F-series.
They popped toward lonely signals or empty fry,
the odd ugly blast when no one registered anything
but the lack of refrigerant in the A.C. It was still
those cool cans of freon back then. Somehow it was
o.k. for me to sweat out sickness on the passenger's
floor-mat the whole way back across Mississippi.

On video, the Very Large Array nods and nods out,
its nodes in heavy unison. Twenty-seven antennae
set to listen for masers and black holes, attuned
to supernova remnants. The rare official car
slowly patrols sun-cracked roads among them.

I'm told my cubical reverberates in serial bleats
of that eerie 90s office ring. Every tinny robocall
timeshifts to voicemail and is marked unheard.

Break in for anything is what most cars convey
when left unattended. What's left of the stereo
is wormed out optic nerve. Limp, with no eye.
Some wires must have crossed themselves
in the violence, otherwise how would the battery
have drained enough to subdue the alarm like that?

Its whisper is a barely broadcast plea: *Get close.*
Kneel down. Close your eyes. It's familiar and
somehow sad: vibrato squeal, inverse squeal,
UK siren, upward sweep, octuple buzzer dash
and rest, repeat repeat repeat repeat.

Under Armor

Ingot, I-beam, rebar, rut.
Sunken tracks in Culebra Cut.
Pig iron, girder, slug and rail.
Melt the bars, empty the jails.

Heavy water, laser rot.
The Terminator Liquid Cop's
On security at the velvet rope.
There's mercury in Gatorade says coach.

In a metallic ceremony,
young & unkempt,
we took on the city
but mostly temped.

III

I'm Not The Cosmos

Never pick a fight with anyone
who still buys blank media in bulk.

Remember the bliss of auto-reverse,
the occult trope of tape hiss in mega-bass.

Underpass, BB gun, something with flame
& acid. Breath or wind rides bodies to the ground.

Some of us only live in cleanses
or rebirths via the jaws of life.

Do me a favor and draw me
your skull real quick. Rewild it.

Every school bus on Long Island sits empty today,
their single seatbelts for drivers only.

As someone old shopvacs the empty houses,
a teen lawnmows trash into scraps for sparkle.

WYSIWYG

Every journey's undergirt
with easy links to the flood

of dumb text a few welcome,
but most ignore by now.

You can watch the little digits
swell to tell it: *deal*, they say;

act. You must. Empire
Service is full of moments

when children become cargo;
they are bundled and huddled

as the dunes of busted dishes
behind the China factory scroll by.

It's a preview, really, only
orderless. Each city is seen

as if caught by surprise, paused
on events no one thought to pick

up for. Ask about these landmarks,
my money says no one replies.

In City Parks, In the Sour Void

I am seven skulls screaming
about seven smaller screaming skulls.

Please take my boney hand &
Celine Dion my sinking ship.

In the capharnaum of microplastics
an animal vigils a similar corpse.

By 25 I had figured out fire
but not much else: anatomy

for interior designers, how to schedule
an unaffiliated neurotrama consultant.

On night ops from null, a prereq
for the living arts, I remember

how payphones once told us
to wait and listen. Meanwhile, we dig.

Magnavox, 1986

My early experiments in blown speaker
magnet exposure summoned yolks

to any image and bent back the spine
of any character I chose. Eventually our set

was acutely symptomatic. A dark cloud
spread across every broadcast to come.

We watched a paramecium of dug-out blur
flit across the shuttle's path as it bloomed

and split toward the corners of the screen
each time. We saw a thick brow of navy

quiver over every portrait of the crew.

Dear Process

If I'm being honest I prefer the other
travelers' magic to my own.

I saw a little girl trying to fill the ocean
with sand. Trust me, she was making progress.

I was on my way back up to the rental cottage
we filled with sand on accident.

Someone bought my medium-tall evening
row-mate a beer he switched to whisky.

I perform extreme frustration with the *USA
Today* from just outside my hotel room door.

I will never write a poem as good as the lists
of words my audiologist makes me say to a wall.

Remember when everyone was able to ignore
the world was basically an ashtray

for every photo op? We set to preserve a single sense.
Now I only have souvenirs from the cities I forgot

to bring a bottle opener to. That's it.

Chorus Distortion

In the late 90s when we all worked
behind a coffee counter & overwrote

our dull codes in a spiralbound shift journal,
I never knew who was doing all the dying.

Before the ink was dry or blurred, we were
already inscrutable as an editorial cartoon

on agebrown paper in an unsealed house. No one
thought of the lost dollars themselves.

We spent evenings criminalizing sacred tasks,
jumping off bikes toward bushes when spooked

by unexpected lights. We penciled in the nights
we'd relapse to flee the neardawn zeitgeist.

There's a thrill in a halfspoon of Purocaff,
& a small amount of surgical risk. *They call that*

dawning realism, it's normal, she said. *It's how*
we eventually become aware of an otherworld.

Whenever you destroy something you know
exactly what questions you can no longer answer.

How golden is your silence? How permanent
your name? Stock photos anticipate every dark scene

played later for laughs in the boardroom or lounge.

Gravity

Our seatback screens synchronize
themselves and pause

on the channel airing a special
on airline disasters:

docucollaged collisions, near misses,
unplanned landings, incidents of debris

re-enacted and soundtracked
by uncalm transmissions from the unnamed

air traffic controllers.
An explosion cascades

through our cabin, among the headrests
and headsetted heads: the pixelated blast

of a zoomed photograph outmooding
any bulbs still lit overhead.

The screens melt together,
dimming in the aisle, oozing

through the spaces between seats
bouncing an aftward blur off the windows,

over tray-table glows, the aura of every
open book. Outside, our fuselage is a stripe

of flickering frames beneath a dull moon.
Our silent shadow falls still on a sheet

of smooth cloud like the amber spots
streetlamps drop onto empty parking lots.

Whatever Falls

From cars whatever falls
look paused as you pass.

On foot you see them pulse,
gush dumping hills behind the rails.

On foot they seem filmed,
not blurry bursts of still.

But try to grip the dopplered roars
of those cars & trucks. You can't,

not from the shoulder.
Some may honk, some hurl cans.

All their stares pan perpendicular
to grab sly glances on passing.

Some old glacier in advance
or retreat cut these walls.

The lake trough's deepest
cracks half-filled with silt.

With each falls, a slew
of continuous debris drags

unseen toward that certain place,
along with whatever falls you miss.

Outside Avon

Disparate cornstalk tips transmit
topography as fluid contour in wind.

Thumb-thick weeds turn tree
and take eyesore homes wholly.

Ivy-climbed silos cede eyeshare,
drop their domes, and near disappear.

Bales protrude as pinion teeth
held still by loamy torque beneath.

Matte-beige tanks rust to betray
ancient leaks and recent rain.

In shaky hand at ladder's height:
Solution to Oil Spill "PRAY."

On a junction billboard: *Cherish Life
Heartbeat 18 days.*

Trace Latex

Bubbles of aging air
fill the fingertips

of a discarded surgical
glove

anonymously haunting
the surface of the brown river.

A couple of condoms
in full unfurl

glide lakewardly by.
A city is built, it erodes

into relics. They photodegrade
in warm water

and fix us forever
in neutonic purgatory.

IV

Conditioning

To the junior high
bio teacher,
who encouraged
birds to enter
his childhood

bedroom
and treated us
as Pavlov's dogs,
forever

poisoning
a certain register
of bell to elicit
mimetic *cherry pies*:

When now, if I must
professionally don
a commemorative t
over shirt and tie,

I pretend I am you.

In essence, you said,
the ones who evolve
are merely those
who happen to last

when everyone else

is busy failing
to survive.

On Departing

We men
were gifted
switchblades.

On each, a bump
to lock, a thumb
to the hilt
to fold its blade.

Mine broke
with decorum
in the back
of a Metropolitan
Avenue taxicab.

Left the avocado
leatherette in shreds,
a lime whose rind
was scarred for twists.

It's never bad
to be the first
to leave, we say,
over and over again.

Every Eyelid Has Two Sides

When we rode in borrowed
clothes and your horse pulled
you oh so far from me,
I should have thought of eyelids.

Instead, I took a your picture:
small, but so distinct against
that snow-masked lavaplain.
Safety orange head to toe.
I couldn't see your tears, frozen
and congruent to every nearby pixel.

Jonathan would always turn
his eyelids inside out in school,
to make us laugh in quiet time.
He taught me mumblety-peg
out front once his mother'd gone.
A cherished chance to maybe hurt
each other, but in a brave way.

When I see myself blink in video
delay, I think of gripping my teeth
on the edge of front and back seat,
tasting the burgundy vinyl piping
of our primer-gray Volare's bench.

We wore shirts backwards
for paints. We played at dentist or
veterinarian. We watched the crows

trash our campsite from half a mile
off shore. Binoculars never flicker;
they only gaze and lay in wait.

Big Money for Broken Gold

You find out what kind
of neighborhood you've got
by how the others jump
when you pass them
on the sidewalks.

In ours, they're almost all
resigned to being
overtaken by surprise.

If you want to know their secrets,
hang out behind the hotel
where the employees
all sneak smokes.

When next we see those idle dads
shredding by sunset at the trashed
skatepark, let's make a pact
to never jump again.

Her ring was diagnosed
nine karats British dull,
and I thought right, the rationing.

Your grandmother's story is
never not achingly everything.

Necessary Facilities Improvements

Here's the gougey bodega,
the graying gym shoe power lines,
sloping toward what television
tells me is our drug corner.

Out front I ghosted through
the earliest blossoms of an ugly
fistfight and didn't look back
until I knew it was over.

Yards away a wet sweatshirt
cloaked a cat's corpse for most
of a winter, until they vanished:
first the sweatshirt, then the cat,
and then, at last, the winter.

In June, someone stole a chandelier,
some stained-glass windows,
and a pair of marble candlesticks
from a home just blocks up Oak.

When the owner returned mid-heist,
the thief faked a search for his lost
cat as he fled. Neighbors blamed
the *For Sale* sign, but they're all
for sale if they're standing around here.

Now that the school has opened again,
I wonder, what stories do the children tell
about this dead end block
from the safety of their schoolyard swings?

Let's Do The Time Weft Again

When we summon,
via demonyms, Karl Marx
or Betamax, we'll see:

In the future we are the ghosts
of every other ether in there,
we are at once each leaver in reverse:

As I am looking through you
you emerge from a hidden drive
at your temporary age:

Your riverine qualities, your
pirate's pirouette best measured
in international bitterness units:

Chording through the newest
dystopia you want to laser away.
Howling and glowing,

then dimming slightly,
and howling again because death
laid an egg.

Night Game

The unspectators patrol their orbits—the field,
the loge, the cheapest seats—casting upward
stares as eighty thousand, post-frisk,
struggle with the climb in full network glow.

They figure brinks of fights, step absently
between sides and ride out drones.
They chart back arcs for whatever's thrown
in the crescendos to third-and-anythings.

The visitors absorb it with what passes
for grace, until you meet their eyes: it's quiet
rage banked away on off chance
their own home seats come through.

Out past the doused grills and pallet fires,
someone ejected's facedown in Smokes Creek.
Toxins waft low and sting the eyes of anyone still
searching as the last traffic is flagged away.

Lanterna

The newer glow is you
struggling to ignite
the ancient bottle gas fixture.

Our lake's shimmer
on the single pane dims
implausibly.

From the screen porch,
my portrait is a scrim-
trick, flush.

Some propane takes your flame.
A glob blooms upward
over you, burns back
the vaporous arbor. It's dusk.

Come dawn we'll see
we left it lit all night.
Somewhere across the lake
someone's known all along.

Monkey Jungle Flashback

My left shoe's somewhere else,
back where I caught cuts off
iron-brown reeds, took some
risks bellydown in pisswarm
muck, groping for shells out
of boredom, to skip the NASCAR.
On the trampoline, with butter
knives, we chipped inexpertly.
With work, even true stubborns
opened up. Doused palms in Texas
Pete before each dicey slurp.
Then back to drop another batch
of room-temp turkeynecks off
an absent neighbor's dock. Under
a bed sheet for sunscreen, relying
on pure feel. Toward dusk, back out
at camp, we dined on buried beans
and got completely inarticulate.
Weird how it all surfaces so often,
in waves of inopinate guilt and vigor.

Loop Current

Out in the Gulf, something
like a day and a half off
Grand Isle, there's this rift
that if it were a shift in dirt,
they'd call it a fault. It's all
we can talk about, the way
bits of old garbage surface
to nuzzle and linger there.
No one can explain it, so
our eyes move to the clouds,
to books about the clouds.
You get to staring at the water,
the sky. There's nothing else
to see until dark, until the oil
rigs light up, until lightning
shows them backlit, too near.
One looms static to port. Down
below, my father's got our backs
to it as he clasps my teenage
hand and rivals its stillness.
You gun our old single diesel
into each deepening swell.
It groans all night *relent.*

Sea Lust

Sea lust ran in families, even those far from the sea.
Find a river, an island. Spend time there learning to sew
your new wounds closed. Breathe into the stillness of pain,
it's got nowhere else to go. Sea lust is not a modern
problem. Sea lust is a dream. Sea lust is a feeling beyond
the loves we commit to greeting cards, beyond the knowing
where something will go or where it will take you. When one
is days from seeing land, or even just setting foot on land,
one must decide: Do I wish to become to the sea? Everything
out here is the sea, even the air has sea in it. Take a smell.
Whoever decides they do not wish to become to the sea
should know they will never learn that still way of breathing,
of having nowhere else to go. Imagine that: you're out there,
somewhere you have been taken, or somewhere you've been sent,
breathing in sea just like you breathe in everything else.

The Broken Record I Want to Sound Like

The broken record I want to sound like is shattered,
but it is also warped. It is also in New Jersey, and
it is only an idea.

The broken record I want to sound like is important,
but it was panned by most critics. It is also the darling
of tomorrow's top critics, if they happen to be born.

The broken record I want to sound like is time-based,
but its pieces have been stacked atop one another,
representing *now*.

The broken record I want to sound like is exasperating,
but it also gives life. It is also pill-shaped, and
is hidden among other pill-shaped things.

The broken record I want to sound like is silent,
but only for the moment, while we wait for machinery
to be built to play it.

The broken record I want to sound like is distasteful,
but it is what others expect of me. It is also outside
of my control.

The broken record I want to sound like is predictable,
it has a beginning, a middle, and an end. It is also
locked away in storage closet at a school closed years ago.

The broken record I want to sound like is growing,

but at a rate microseconds slower
than everything else. It is also turning to dust.

The broken record I want to sound like is hexagonal,
but I've only seen it through a kaleidoscope. Someone
told me that makes it more real.

The broken record I want to sound like is arbitrary,
and contains mostly static. It also contains encoded plans
for a machine to dilate strangers' eyes.

The broken record I want to sound like is tender,
but it is in a shabby sleeve. It is also at risk
of being overlooked completely.

The broken record I want to sound like is catastrophic,
it includes a list of names left out of the official
report. It is also slightly warmer than the space around it.

The broken record I want to sound like is faith-based,
but its biggest fans explain that away. It is also laying
on top of an unused Yellow Pages.

The broken record I want to sound like is split,
so rather than two sides, it has four sides. It is also
sensitive to light.

The broken record I want to sound like is dull,
but it is also long, so no one really notices. It drives
audiences into themselves, then it steals their wallets.

The broken record I want to sound like is cheerful.
It is uplifting, really. No one wants it to end.
Also, it never ends.

The broken record I want to sound like is public,
but you have to sign a waiver to view it. It is also
the thing in the museum they bought the velvet ropes for.

The broken record I want to sound like is listening,
but it doesn't react or respond. Not because it doesn't care,
but because it is saving up anecdotes for a screenplay.

The broken record I want to sound like is frozen.
It came that way, inside a clear block of ice. It is
heavier than regular ice. And also colder.

The broken record I want to sound like is beautiful,
but it is also unsavory, thanks to the symbols someone
scratched onto its surface. I try to hide them with my coat.

The broken record I want to sound like is spacious,
but it is closed most weekends in the spring. They call
it *maintenance season*, but they also laugh when they say that.

The broken record I want to sound like is lifelike,
but in a not-unsettling way. No one suspects it will
hop of the shelf at night and wander through the house.

The broken record I want to sound like is swollen,
something about the wood-pulp, or the humidity,
or the fact that it's mostly made of skin.

The broken record I want to sound like is *"electric,"*
but "electric" in scare quotes, which has me thinking
it's not electric at all.

The broken record I want to sound like is ugly evidence,
but it has other redeeming qualities that make it
the must-have item this holiday season.

Afterlife

I hope my Anubis will come
in the form of an old-stock
Radio Shack Bulk Tape Eraser.
Unboxed, plugged in, it needn't
even touch the decades-old
emulsion holding our play-act
broadcasts so insecurely. A tasteful
funerary implosion is what I have
in mind: any traces on old discs
degaussed into a ghost spiral
of gone. Aging magnetic tape
wrapped tight on geared plastic
spools, slung slack across that
tan cube of foam, all shot through
with a dry rumble. That's it. Every
bit since year zero, day zero
disannulled regardless of filename
or source. It worked so well
on those gimme Bonnie Raitt
cassingles. They're dusty now,
resonant with tweaked-out
metronome, but with luck,
not for long. The goal is to be equal
parts lossy and inarticulate.